How To Understand The Human Psychology:

Investigating, Recognizing, and Anticipating Emotions, Thoughts, Intentions, and Behaviors.

By

DR. EMMA EMERALD

CONTENTS

PREFACE

Step into the enthralling realm of "How To Understand The Human Psychology: Investigating, Recognizing, and Anticipating Emotions, Thoughts, Intentions, and Behaviors." In this expedition, we set out to untangle the intricate threads of the human mind, exploring the depths of emotions, thoughts, intentions, and behaviors that shape our daily existence.

This book acts as a guide through the diverse landscapes of psychology, catering to both novices and seasoned explorers of the human psyche. Our journey kicks off by delving into the intricacies of cognitive processes and patterns, deciphering how our minds construct thoughts and emotions in our day-to-day lives.

As we navigate through the multifaceted terrain of cognitive biases, technological strides, and interdisciplinary approaches, each chapter unfurls a new facet of human psychology. Real-life examples shed light on the practical applications of psychological principles, illustrating the relevance of our understanding in contexts ranging from therapy rooms to crime investigations.

Our gaze extends beyond the present, foreseeing upcoming trends that are set to reshape the field of psycho-social understanding. Technological progress, ethical considerations, and the amalgamation of diverse disciplines sketch a picture of the evolving landscape, urging readers to contemplate the exciting possibilities that lie ahead.

In the spirit of continuous learning, this book fosters an open-minded exploration of psychological concepts. Whether you are a student, a practitioner, or simply curious, the goal is to provide a road-map for investigating the intricacies of human psychology and recognizing the myriad influences on our thoughts, emotions, and behaviors.

As you immerse yourself in these pages, embrace the journey of understanding human psychology as a dynamic and ever-unfolding adventure. May this exploration kindle curiosity, inspire insights, and contribute to a deeper understanding of the captivating world within each of us. Welcome to the exhilarating quest of unraveling the mysteries and wonders of the human mind.

PART I

INTRODUCTION

Embarking on the journey into the depths of human psychology opens doors to a profound comprehension of what drives individuals, shapes their perceptions, and influences their actions. In this exploration, we delve into the intricate tapestry of emotions, thoughts, intentions, and behaviors, aiming to unravel the mysteries that define human nature. This comprehensive guide seeks to equip individuals with the tools to investigate, recognize, and anticipate the nuanced aspects of psychology, fostering a deeper understanding that transcends interpersonal connections and extends into various facets of professional and personal life. Join us as we navigate the complexities of the human mind, unraveling the threads that connect us all in this captivating exploration of the human psyche.

This excursion isn't simply a scholastic pursuit however a viable undertaking with sweeping ramifications. Figuring out the unobtrusive signs of feelings, unraveling the complexities of contemplation, knowing expectations, and foreseeing ways of behaving are abilities that engage people in assorted settings. Whether exploring the complexities of individual connections, upgrading group elements in the work environment, or going with very much educated choices in different expert settings, the capacity to get a handle on the nuances of human brain science turns into a directing compass.

As we embark on this exploration, we will navigate through the realms of cognitive processes, emotional landscapes, and behavioral patterns. By shedding light on psychological models, ethical considerations, and real-world case studies, we aim to provide a road-map for honing the invaluable skill of decoding the human experience.

In a world where effective communication, empathy, and insight are currency, the knowledge gleaned from investigating human psychology becomes a powerful tool. Join us in unraveling the layers of the human psyche, as we strive to not only understand ourselves better but also to foster a more harmonious and insightful coexistence with those around us.

CHAPTER 1:

Importance of Understanding Human Psychology

Comprehending human psychology goes beyond academic pursuits; it serves as a cornerstone for personal development, effective communication, and success across diverse life domains. The importance of this understanding can be outlined as follows:

1. Deepened Self-Insight:

Exploring human psychology offers individuals profound insights into their thoughts, emotions, and behaviors, fostering personal growth and a comprehensive understanding of one's motivations.

2. Fortified Relationships:

Whether in personal or professional spheres, the ability to comprehend others' emotions, thoughts, and intentions cultivates empathy and strengthens relationships. Effective communication and conflict resolution become more attainable when navigating the intricacies of human behavior.

3. Leadership Acumen:

Leaders and managers benefit significantly from a robust understanding of human psychology, facilitating efficient team management, motivation, and the foresight to address the needs of team members.

4. Informed Decision-Making:

Decisions in various fields are often shaped by human behavior. Understanding the psychology behind decision-making equips individuals to make well-informed choices, both personally and professionally.

5. Effective Stress Handling:

Proficiency in managing personal stress and discerning stressors in others contributes to a healthier environment, particularly in workplaces and interpersonal relationships.

6. Conflict Resolution Skills:

Conflict is inherent in human interactions, and understanding its root causes, coupled with effective resolution strategies, enables individuals to navigate disagreements constructively.

7. Social Competency:

In an interconnected society, understanding human psychology is vital for navigating social dynamics, fostering inclusivity, cultural competence, and building cohesive communities.

8. Professional Growth:

Professions across various sectors, including marketing, counseling, education, law enforcement, and healthcare, benefit from a profound understanding of human psychology. Professionals can tailor their approaches based on nuanced insights into human behavior.

In essence, a grasp of human psychology empowers individuals to navigate human interactions with compassion, insight, and adaptability. This foundational skill contributes not only to personal success but also to the overall well-being of communities and societies.

.

CHAPTER 2:
Scope of Investigating Emotions, Thoughts, Intentions, and Behaviors

Studying how people feel, think, plan, and act is like taking a deep dive into human behavior. Let's break it down:

1. Emotions:

A. Diversity: Understanding all the different feelings people have, from basic to complex.

B. Expression: Figuring out how people show their emotions, whether by talking, body language, or other ways.

C. Cultural Impact: Seeing how where someone comes from influences how they feel and express emotions.

2. Thoughts:

A. Cognitive Processes: Checking out how our minds work – how we see things, remember stuff, solve problems, make decisions, and think critically.

B. Cognitive Biases: Realizing that our thoughts can be influenced by personal biases and how we see things subjectively.

3. Intentions:

A. Communication Analysis: Trying to understand why people say and do things by looking at both what they say and how they say it, whether it's in personal relationships, at work, or in the wider world.

B. Motivational Factors: Finding out what drives people to do what they do and make certain decisions.

4. Behaviors:

A. Observable Actions: Watching what people do, how they react, and the patterns in how they behave in different situations.

B. Environmental Influences: Understanding how outside factors like rules or surroundings can affect how people act.

C. Predictive Analysis: Figuring out what someone might do based on past observations and what we know about psychology.

5. Interconnectedness:

A. Integration of Elements: Realizing that emotions, thoughts, intentions, and behaviors are all connected. Changes in one can affect the others, making human psychology like a dynamic puzzle.

B. Holistic Approach: Looking at the big picture when studying these things together, giving a complete view of how they all work together.

6. Technological Advances:

A. Data Analytics: Using fancy technology to analyze lots of information and find patterns in how people feel, think, plan, and act.

B. Neuroscientific Insights: Using tools like brain scans to learn more about the biological side of how our emotions and thoughts work.

In short, exploring how people feel, think, plan, and act goes beyond just looking at one thing. It's like solving a puzzle that helps us understand the complex world of human behavior in different areas like psychology, sociology, business, education, and more.

PART II

The Basics of Human Emotions

Welcome to the foundational exploration of human emotions – an intriguing journey into the very essence of what makes us human. In this exploration, we will unravel the common feelings that color our daily experiences, understand how these emotions manifest in our bodies and behaviors, appreciate the diversity of emotional expressions among individuals and cultures, explore the evolution and development of our emotional landscape, and recognize the interconnected nature that weaves the tapestry of our emotional experiences.

In essence, Part II serves as an extensive exploration into the fundamental aspects of human emotions. By deconstructing common feelings, scrutinizing their visible manifestations, acknowledging individual and cultural influences, understanding developmental dynamics, exploring evolutionary roots, and recognizing interconnectedness, we gain profound insights into the complex and evolving world of human emotions. This knowledge not only enhances self-awareness but also cultivates empathy and emotional intelligence, empowering us to navigate the rich complexities of our shared human experience.

Join us as we delve into the basics of human emotions, unlocking insights that enhance our self-awareness and enrich our understanding of the complex world of feelings.Exploring the core elements of human emotions, we unravel the complex realm of feelings that define our daily lives and contribute to the essence of humanity.

CHAPTER 3:
Overview of Emotions

At the heart of the human emotional experience lies a spectrum of emotions that color our perceptions and interactions. These include joy, sadness, anger, fear, surprise, and disgust. Each emotion plays a distinct role in our lives, contributing to the rich tapestry of human feelings. Understanding these common emotions serves as a foundational element, allowing us to navigate the complexity of our emotional landscape.

A. Various Emotions:

At the heart of our emotional spectrum are familiar sensations such as joy, sadness, anger, fear, surprise, and disgust. These emotions act as primary colors on the canvas of our internal experiences, forming the basis for a comprehensive understanding of our emotional landscape.

B. Expression of Emotions:

Emotions are not silent; they leave visible marks on our bodies and behaviors. Facial expressions, body language, and physiological responses, such as changes in heart rate, serve as observable cues. These indicators offer insights into the intricate orchestra of our emotional states, enriching our ability to interpret our emotions and empathize with others.

C. Diversity in Individuals:

Uniqueness plays a pivotal role in how we encounter and convey emotions. This section explores the impact of personal backgrounds and cultural contexts on emotional diversity. Recognizing and valuing these differences deepen our grasp of emotions, showcasing the myriad ways individuals navigate their emotional worlds.

D. Evolution of Emotions:

Emotions are dynamic, evolving as we traverse the journey of life. From the instinctual reactions of infancy to the nuanced expressions of adulthood, this segment delves into the developmental facets of emotions. Acknowledging the transformative nature of emotions over time enhances our comprehension of emotional intelligence and maturation.

E. Purpose of Emotions:

Emotions possess a purpose deeply rooted in our evolutionary past. This section probes into the adaptive significance of emotions, elucidating why certain feelings are integral to our human experience. Understanding the evolutionary role of emotions adds layers to our appreciation for the intricate interplay between our emotional responses and survival instincts.

F. Interconnected Nature of Emotions:

Emotions seldom exist in isolation; they intertwine and influence one another. This segment scrutinizes how emotions connect, crafting a dynamic emotional fabric. Whether it involves the coexistence of joy and sadness or the shift from fear to relief, recognizing the interconnected nature of emotions provides a holistic viewpoint on the intricate tapestry of our emotional experiences.

CHAPTER 4:

Physiological and Behavioral Indicators

Deciphering the Expressive Language of Emotions. Explore the intricate language of emotions not articulated in words but revealed through the silent signals of our bodies and behaviors. This section delves into how emotions physically and behaviorally manifest, offering profound insights into the depth of our inner world.

A. Facial Expressions:

Our faces act as dynamic canvases, painting a vivid picture of our emotional states. Whether it's a smile of joy, furrowed brows denoting concern, or a frown expressing displeasure, these facial expressions form a universal language, transcending cultural boundaries.

B. Body Language:

Beyond facial cues, our bodies become storytellers of emotions. Posture, movement, and gestures convey a wealth of information. A slouched posture might communicate sadness, while lively gestures express excitement or enthusiasm.

C. Physiological Responses:

Emotions leave an imprint on our physical well-being. Accelerated heartbeats, changes in breathing, or pupil dilation are physiological indicators of our emotional state. These subtle cues provide an internal road-map, aiding our understanding of emotions on a visceral level.

D. Verbal Communication:

While words carry emotional weight, the tone, pitch, and pace of our voice contribute emotional nuances. A soft tone may convey comfort, while a sharp tone indicates frustration. Recognizing these auditory cues enhances our ability to perceive the emotional undertones in communication.

E. Micro-expressions:

Fleeting and involuntary, micro-expressions are brief facial expressions occurring in a fraction of a second. These micro-moments unveil authentic emotions before conscious control. Understanding these subtle cues sharpens our interpretation of emotions.

Delving into the physiological and behavioral indicators of emotions, we embark on a journey to decode the unspoken language bridging our internal emotional experiences with external expressions. This exploration not only amplifies our understanding of personal emotions but also deepens our comprehension of the unarticulated emotions exhibited by those around us.

PART III

Recognizing Thoughts and Cognitive Patterns

Welcome to the third segment of our exploration – an intriguing voyage into the domain of cognition and thought processes. In this section, we will unravel the complex intricacies of the human mind, exploring the captivating landscape of thoughts, reasoning, and cognitive patterns. By acknowledging the subtle threads that intricately shape our cognitive processes, we embark on a journey to comprehend how our minds influence our perceptions, decisions, and the very core of our intellectual existence. Join us as we delve into the captivating world of recognizing thoughts and cognitive patterns, uncovering insights that illuminate the intricacies of human cognition.

In Part III, we delve into the intricate landscape of recognizing thoughts and cognitive patterns. Exploring the nuanced ways in which our minds process information, this section aims to unravel the mysteries of human cognition. From identifying thought patterns to understanding the underlying mechanisms that shape our mental landscape.

Part III is a journey into the fascinating realm of introspection and self-awareness. we delve into the intricate workings of our cognitive processes, unraveling the complexities of thought recognition and the patterns that influence our perceptions and behaviors. This section serves as a guide for readers seeking a profound understanding of self-awareness and the subtle interplay of thoughts that shape our daily lives.

CHAPTER 5:

Cognitive Processes and Patterns

Exploring cognitive processes entails a comprehensive examination of the intricate mental operations that underpin human cognition. Elements such as perception, attention, memory, language, problem-solving, and decision-making collectively constitute the complex landscape of cognitive functions. Researchers across psychology, neuroscience, and artificial intelligence delve into these processes to unravel the intricacies of human thought and behavior.

Cognitive patterns, as recurring sequences of these processes, offer insights into how individuals navigate their surroundings. These patterns develop over time, shaping how people approach tasks and challenges. From a detail-oriented focus to a holistic perspective, the diversity of cognitive patterns influences our interactions with the environment.

Understanding cognitive processes and patterns has practical implications across diverse fields. In education, recognizing varied cognitive patterns aids in tailoring teaching methods to suit different learning styles. Effective communication is also contingent on acknowledging and adapting to the cognitive patterns prevalent in diverse audiences.

The exploration of cognitive processes and patterns intersects with artificial intelligence, aiming to replicate human-like thinking in machines. By integrating cognitive models into AI systems, developers strive to enhance problem-solving, refine natural language understanding, and improve decision-making processes.

As technological advancements progress, incorporating cognitive insights into AI raises ethical considerations. Delving into the ethical dimensions of replicating cognitive processes in machines becomes paramount as we navigate the evolving landscape of artificial intelligence.

In essence, the investigation into cognitive processes and patterns is a dynamic journey spanning psychology, education, technology, and ethics. It not only enriches our comprehension of the human mind but also shapes our interaction with advancing technologies that increasingly emulate cognitive functions. These are;

A. Memory Operations:

Explanation: Memory processes encompass the stages of acquiring, storing, and recalling information. Encoding transforms sensory input into a memory-compatible format, storage preserves it over time, and retrieval brings it back into conscious awareness. Cognitive tendencies related to memory may differ, impacting how individuals remember and utilize information. Some may prioritize detailed recall, while others focus on broader concepts.

B. Approaches to Problem-Solving:

Explanation: Problem-solving involves using information and skills to achieve a goal or overcome challenges. Various problem-solving patterns exist, including analytical problem-solving, characterized by a systematic approach, and intuitive problem-solving, relying on instinctual feelings. Cognitive patterns in problem-solving influence an individual's strategy, emphasizing logical analysis or creative thinking based on past experiences and learned methods.

C. Attentional Operations:

Explanation: Attention is the cognitive process determining which information from the environment is selected for further processing. Cognitive patterns linked to attention exhibit diversity. Some individuals demonstrate sustained attention, staying focused on a task for an extended period, while others display selective attention, concentrating on specific aspects of a situation. Attentional processes profoundly shape how individuals perceive and engage with their surroundings.

Grasping these cognitive processes and patterns yields insights into the nuances of individual thinking and behavior. Interconnected and influential in learning, decision-making, and daily navigation, these processes allow researchers and educators to customize interventions, educational strategies, and communication methods to accommodate diverse cognitive preferences and enhance overall cognitive functioning.

CHAPTER 6:

Identifying Cognitive Biases

Spotting how our thinking might go off track is crucial. Cognitive biases are like predictable patterns that can affect how we judge things or make decisions. Knowing these biases not only helps us understand ourselves better but also makes our decision-making better. Here's a simpler take on recognizing a few of these biases:

A. Confirmation Bias:

We tend to like information that agrees with what we already think and ignore what disagrees. To recognize this, try to listen to different ideas and think about other points of view.

B. Availability Heuristic:

Sometimes, we make decisions based on what comes to our mind easily, even if it's not the best info. To catch this, try to look for more information and not just rely on what's right in front of you.

C. Anchoring Bias:

We often rely too much on the first piece of information we get. To notice this, think if that first bit of info is really the most important, and be open to changing your mind.

D. Overconfidence Bias:

We might think we're better at things than we really are. To see this, be honest with yourself about what you know and don't know. It's okay not to know everything!

E. Sunk Cost Fallacy:

Sometimes, we stick with something just because we already put time or effort into it, even if it's not the best choice. To avoid this, ask yourself if it still makes sense to keep going or if it's better to stop and try something else.

Seeing these biases is an ongoing thing. It's about paying attention to how you think, being open to feedback, and trying to make decisions with a clear and fair mindset. Understanding these biases helps you make better choices in different parts of your life.

PART IV

Investigating Intentions

Investigating intentions involves a thoughtful exploration into the motives behind actions or decisions. This process seeks to uncover the underlying reasons that drive individuals or entities to behave in a certain way. By delving into intentions, we aim to gain a deeper understanding of the thought processes, goals, and values influencing human behavior. This investigative journey often entails examining verbal and non-verbal cues, considering past behaviors, and evaluating the context surrounding an action. Ultimately, investigating intentions provides valuable insights for decision-making, interpersonal relationships, and navigating complex situations with a nuanced perspective.

Embarking on the inquiry into intentions opens the gateway to understanding the intricate motivations steering human actions. It involves peeling away layers to discern the unseen forces that mold our choices and interactions. Intentions, like imperceptible threads, intricately weave through the fabric of our lives, molding our decisions and behaviors. This exploration encompasses deciphering the language of motives, untangling the complexities that lie beneath our actions.

In this venture, we grapple with the challenge of distinguishing authentic motivations from surface-level expressions. Unraveling intentions requires a mix of empathy, perception, and analytical skills, delving into the subtle cues and subconscious drivers shaping our behavior. Investigating intentions is not just a quest born out of curiosity; it stands as a vital pursuit for building understanding, fostering trust, and making well-informed judgments in personal and professional domains.

Recognizing that intentions are multifaceted and influenced by diverse factors, including cultural nuances and personal histories, adds richness to this exploration. The art of investigating intentions necessitates a nuanced approach, demanding an awareness of context and a readiness to navigate the intricacies of human nature. Ultimately, gaining insights into intentions equips us to traverse the complex web of human interactions with discernment and compassion.

CHAPTER 7:
Non-verbal Cues and Communication

Non-verbal cues are like a secret language in communication, making spoken words even more powerful. These cues include things like gestures, facial expressions, and how we use our bodies and voices. Understanding them helps us connect better with others.

1. Body Language:

Our body language, like gestures and how we stand, shows our feelings and intentions. Paying attention to these cues lets us understand emotions that words might not fully express.

2. Facial Expressions:

Our faces tell a story through smiles, frowns, or raised eyebrows. Recognizing these expressions helps us figure out how someone feels during a conversation.

3. Eye Contact:

Looking someone in the eyes is a powerful way to show we're engaged and sincere. Not keeping eye contact might mean someone is not interested or feels uneasy. Understanding this helps build trust.

4. Tone of Voice:

How we say things, like the pitch and speed of our voice, conveys feelings beyond the words. It helps others understand our emotions and intentions, making communication richer.

5. Cultural Sensitivity:

Different cultures have different non-verbal cues. Being aware of these differences helps prevent misunderstandings and promotes better communication, especially when interacting with people from diverse backgrounds.

In a nutshell, paying attention to non-verbal cues is like learning an extra language. It makes our communication more meaningful, allowing us to connect better with others by understanding their emotions and intentions beyond just words.

CHAPTER 8:
Analyzing Verbal Expressions

Analyzing verbal expressions means more than just hearing words; it's about understanding the feelings, intentions, and extra meanings behind what someone says. This involves paying attention to the words used, the way they're said, and considering the situation and cultural differences. Here are simpler points about why this is important:

1. Choosing Words:

Words can mean more than their usual definition. Analyzing verbal expressions means noticing the specific words and phrases someone uses, which can show how they're feeling or what they really mean.

2. Tone of Voice:

How someone says things, like if they sound excited, annoyed, or caring, gives extra meaning to their words.

Analyzing tone helps understand the emotions behind what's being said.

3. Context Matters:

Understanding verbal expressions is better when you know what's happening around the conversation. It's like putting the words in the right situation to understand them better.

4. Body Language Helps:

Sometimes, people show what they mean not just by words but also by how they move or look. Analyzing both words and body language together gives a clearer picture of what someone is trying to say.

5. Different Cultures, Different Expressions:

In different places, people might use words or expressions differently. Being aware of these differences helps avoid misunderstandings and makes communication better, especially when talking to people from other backgrounds.

6. Understanding Feelings:

Analyzing verbal expressions also means understanding how someone feels. It's like noticing not just the words but also the emotions behind them.

7. Listening Well:

Good listening is a big part of understanding verbal expressions. It's about paying attention, repeating what you heard, and asking questions to make sure you get what someone is saying.

In simple terms, analyzing verbal expressions is like reading between the lines when someone talks. It's about not just hearing words but understanding the feelings, meanings, and situations that make communication richer and more meaningful.

PART V

Behavioral Analysis

Behavioral analysis is a systematic and scientific approach to understanding, interpreting, and predicting human behavior. It involves observing and examining actions, reactions, and patterns to uncover valuable insights into an individual's thoughts, motivations, and intentions. This method employs various techniques from psychology, criminology, and other disciplines to analyze behavioral cues, providing a comprehensive understanding of why people act the way they do. From deciphering non-verbal signals to investigating decision-making processes, behavioral analysis serves as a powerful tool in diverse fields such as psychology, law enforcement, and organizational management, contributing to a deeper comprehension of human actions and aiding in informed decision-making.

Behavioral analysis is like a detective work for understanding why people do what they do. It's a methodical way of observing and figuring out patterns in how individuals behave. By looking at how people act and react, behavioral analysis helps uncover the reasons behind their actions, thoughts, and intentions.

This approach uses insights from psychology, crime studies, and other fields to decode behavior. Whether it's used in understanding mental health, profiling criminals, or improving teamwork in organizations, behavioral analysis is a versatile tool. It looks closely at both what people say and how they act, offering a complete picture of individuals and groups.

Behavioral analysis is always evolving, keeping up with advancements in technology and psychology. It not only explains past behavior but also helps predict what someone might do in the future. This field bridges the gap between what we see people do and the reasons behind their actions. From personal development to strategies in law enforcement and leadership, behavioral analysis provides valuable insights into why people behave the way they do.

CHAPTER 9:

Observing and Interpreting Behavior

Watching and understanding how people behave is like uncovering a secret code to their thoughts and feelings. It's a useful skill in psychology, social situations, and everyday life. Here's a simpler breakdown:

1. Getting to Know Feelings:

   By paying attention to how someone acts, you can figure out what they might be feeling. Facial expressions, body language, and gestures show a lot about what's going on in their head.

2. Spotting Repetitive Actions:

   People often do things in a certain way repeatedly. Noticing these patterns helps predict what someone might do next, whether it's reacting to stress or handling specific situations.

3. Respecting Different Cultures:

Different cultures express emotions in different ways. Being aware of these differences helps avoid misunderstandings. It's like considering where someone is from when figuring out what their actions mean.

4. Understanding Without Words:

People communicate not just with words but also with how they look and move. Paying attention to these non-verbal cues helps you understand what someone is trying to say even when they don't say it.

5. Finding Reasons Behind Actions:

People do things for a reason. It could be to get approval, avoid trouble, or achieve personal goals. Understanding why someone acts a certain way helps you get what drives them.

6. Making Communication Better:

Communication is more than just talking. Understanding how people act without words makes it easier for everyone to understand each other. It helps get the full meaning behind what someone says.

7. Helping in Different Jobs:

Understanding behavior is useful in jobs like psychology (helping understand mental health), law enforcement (figuring out criminal behavior), and workplaces (making teams work well together).

8. Getting Along with Others:

Social situations can be tricky, but watching and understanding how people behave helps you get along with others. It makes relationships better and helps you handle social situations more easily.

In simple terms, observing and understanding behavior is like having a superpower to connect with others, make good choices, and navigate the ups and downs of how people act in different situations.

CHAPTER 10:

Factors Influencing Behavior

Why people behave the way they do is influenced by many things. Let's break it down:

1. Born This Way:

Some behaviors are influenced by the way we're born – our genes, brain structure, and chemicals in our brain all play a part. These things make us unique and affect how we act.

2. How We Think and Feel:

The way we think, feel, and our personality also influence our behavior. How we understand things, our emotions, and the kind of person we are all affect the way we act.

3. Friends, Family, and Culture:

Our behavior is shaped by the people around us and the culture we live in. Our family, friends, and society have expectations, and we often learn from watching and copying others.

4. Where We Live:

The place we live, the resources we have, and our surroundings influence our behavior. Things like where we are, what opportunities we have, and what we're exposed to impact the way we act.

5. Growing Up and Changing:

As we grow, our behavior changes. Our experiences as kids, what we learn in school, and important events in our lives all contribute to how we behave over time.

6. Our Personal Stories:

Our own experiences, good and bad, shape our behavior. Things that happened in the past affect how we see the world and make decisions now.

7. Thinking Things Through:

How we think, solve problems, and make decisions is also part of behavior. Our thinking processes influence the choices we make in different situations.

8. Feeling Emotions:

Emotions like happiness, fear, anger, and sadness are a big part of behavior. How we feel in different situations affects what we do and how we react.

9. Money Matters:

Our financial situation, job, and opportunities influence behavior. Money and economic factors affect our lifestyle choices and well-being, impacting how we act.

10. Tech Changes How We Act:

Technology, like phones and computers, changes the way we behave. Social media, for example, influences how we communicate and interact with the world.

11. School Days and Learning:

What we learn in school and our educational experiences also impact behavior. Access to good education and exposure to different ideas shape how we solve problems and make decisions.

Understanding behavior means looking at all these factors together. It shows that behavior is not simple – it's influenced by a mix of things. Exploring these influences helps us understand and deal with the way people act in different situations.

PART VI

Psychological Models and Frameworks

Psychological models and frameworks serve as structured blueprints for understanding the complexities of the human mind and behavior. These conceptual structures provide psychologists and researchers with organized frameworks to explore, explain, and predict various aspects of cognition, emotions, and actions. In essence, they are the scaffolding that supports the study of psychological phenomena, offering a systematic approach to unraveling the intricacies of mental processes and behavior. Let's delve into the diverse world of psychological models and frameworks, where theories and structures provide a road-map for exploring the fascinating landscape of the human psyche.

Psychological models and frameworks form the intellectual backbone of the field, offering comprehensive frameworks that guide our exploration of the human mind. These models serve as conceptual maps, aiding psychologists in navigating the intricate terrain of thoughts, emotions, and behaviors. From classic theories that laid the groundwork for understanding human development to contemporary frameworks incorporating neuroscience and technology, the realm of psychological models is diverse and ever-evolving.

These models provide a structured lens through which we analyze, interpret, and make sense of the complexities that define human psychology. Whether delving into personality traits, cognitive processes, or social interactions, psychological models offer a systematic approach to unraveling the mysteries of the mind. They are not static blueprints but dynamic tools that adapt to new discoveries and changing perspectives, reflecting the evolving nature of psychological inquiry.

In this exploration, we uncover not just theoretical frameworks but practical applications. Psychological models guide therapeutic interventions, inform educational practices, and contribute to organizational psychology, showcasing their relevance in various aspects of our lives. As we journey through this intellectual landscape, we encounter models that range from individual-focused theories to those examining group dynamics, shedding light on the interplay between the individual and the broader social context.

In essence, the study of psychological models and frameworks is an odyssey into the depths of human understanding. It's a quest to unravel the intricacies of our thoughts, emotions, and behaviors, guided by the rich tapestry of theories and structures that have shaped the field of psychology. This journey not only enhances our comprehension of the human experience but also underscores the dynamic nature of psychological inquiry, where models continually evolve to capture the ever-expanding dimensions of the mind.

CHAPTER 11:

Psychologists and Psychodynamic Theories

Alright, let's dive a bit deeper into Psychologists and

Psychodynamic theories using simpler terms.

Psychologists Big Ideas:

Imagine your mind like an iceberg, with a small part visible

(conscious mind) and a huge part hidden underwater

(unconscious mind). Psychologists thought that stuff hiding

in the deep (like memories and desires you might not even

know about) affects how you act and feel.

They also said your mind has three buddies:

- The "id" wants pleasure and is like your wild, impulsive side.

- The "ego" is the thinker, balancing what you want with what's real.

- The "superego" is like your moral compass, telling you right from wrong.

Psychodynamic Pals:

Other psychologists added their ideas. They agreed that what's hidden in your mind influences you but put their spin on it.

Your Unconscious Friend:

Think of your unconscious mind like a friend whispering suggestions in your ear. Sometimes you do things without even realizing why – it's your unconscious friend nudging you.

Feeling Protective:

When things get tough, your mind has defense mechanisms like avoiding thoughts or blaming others. Picture these as mind superheroes, helping you cope with challenges.

Childhood Memories Stick Around:

Remember that embarrassing thing from when you were little? Psychodynamic pals say these memories stick with you and can shape how you behave even as a grown-up.

Therapy Chats:

In therapy, it's like having a chat with a detective looking for clues in your mind. They help you understand why you do certain things and work through any mind puzzles causing trouble.

So, Psychologists and Psychodynamic ideas are like getting to know the backstage of your mind, understanding hidden thoughts, and figuring out why you are the way you are. It's like having a team of mind detectives helping you unravel the mysteries of your own thoughts and behaviors.

CHAPTER 12:

Cognitive-Behavioral Approaches

Cognitive-Behavioral Approaches (CBAs) are like tool-kits that help us understand and improve the way we think, feel, and act. They say our thoughts influence our emotions and behaviors and offer practical ways to change unhelpful patterns. Let's break it down:

The Power of Thoughts:

CBAs focus on how our thoughts can make us feel and act. Imagine your mind telling stories – CBAs help you work on making those stories more positive.

Spotting Unhelpful Thoughts:

CBAs teach us to notice thoughts that aren't helpful. If you catch yourself thinking something like "I always mess up,"

CBAs help you question that thought and think more balanced thoughts.

Changing Negative Patterns:

CBAs help break the cycle of feeling down and having negative thoughts. By changing those negative thoughts, you can make yourself feel better and act in a more positive way.

Doing Actions to Reach Goals:

CBAs are not just about thoughts; they're also about actions. If you're avoiding something because it makes you anxious, CBAs guide you to face it bit by bit, building confidence.

Setting Goals and Solving Problems:

CBAs are big on setting realistic goals and finding solutions. It's like having a plan for where you want to go and tools to overcome problems along the way.

Being Mindful and Present:

CBAs teach staying focused on the present moment. Instead of worrying about the past or future, they help you be here and now, reducing stress.

Therapy Techniques:

CBAs are often used in therapy, where you work with someone to understand and change your thoughts and actions. It's like having a coach for your mind, helping you be your best self.

Flexibility and Adapting:

CBAs are flexible and work for different situations and people. Whether you're dealing with feeling anxious, sad, or just want to feel better, CBAs can be adjusted to fit what you need.

Homework for Your Mind:

CBAs might involve doing exercises outside of therapy. It's like doing homework for your mind, practicing new ways of thinking and acting to make positive habits.

In simple terms, Cognitive-Behavioral Approaches are like mental exercises. They help you understand how your thoughts affect you, change unhelpful thoughts, and build habits that make you feel happier and healthier.

PART VII

Empathy and Emotional Intelligence

Empathy and Emotional Intelligence are like the dynamic duo of understanding and navigating the complex world of feelings. These intertwined qualities are not just about recognizing emotions but also about using that awareness to connect with others on a deeper level. In this exploration, we'll unravel the essence of empathy and emotional intelligence, understanding how they shape relationships, communication, and overall well-being. Get ready to embark on a journey into the heart of emotional understanding and intelligence.

Empathy and Emotional Intelligence stand as pillars in the realm of human connection, fostering a profound understanding of emotions within ourselves and others. In this deeper dive, we'll unravel the intricate tapestry of empathy and emotional intelligence, exploring how these qualities elevate our interactions, empower effective communication, and contribute to the fabric of compassionate and thriving relationships. Brace yourself for a journey into the intricacies of emotional awareness and the skillful navigation of the human experience.

CHAPTER 13:

Developing Empathy

Becoming more empathetic is like getting better at understanding and connecting with others. Here's how you can do it in simpler terms:

1. Listen Well:

When someone talks, really pay attention. Try to understand not just what they're saying but how they're feeling.

2. See Things from Their Side:

Imagine how someone else sees things. It's like stepping into their shoes and understanding their point of view.

3. Be Open-Minded:

Stay open to different ideas and feelings. Everyone is different, and being open-minded helps you understand and appreciate those differences.

4. Share Your Feelings:

Talk about your own feelings. When you're open about how you feel, it encourages others to share their feelings too.

5. Learn About Different Cultures:

Find out about how people from different cultures live. Understanding their traditions and customs helps you relate to them better.

6. Help Out in Your Community:

Get involved in community activities or help others. Doing things for others gives you real experiences that make you more aware of people's needs and feelings.

7. Control Your Emotions:

Learn to manage your own feelings. When you can control your emotions, you're in a better position to understand and help others with theirs.

8. Read and Watch Different Stories:

Enjoy books and movies that tell stories about different people and situations. It broadens your understanding of emotions and helps you relate to others.

9. Show Interest in Others:

Ask questions and show you're interested in others. Being curious about people helps you connect with them and understand their feelings.

10. Think About Your Interactions:

Reflect on how you talk and act around others. Consider how what you say or do might affect their feelings. Being aware of this helps you grow in understanding others.

Remember, getting better at empathy takes practice. Keep trying, and little by little, you'll find that you're better at understanding and connecting with the people around you.

It's like building a skill that makes the world a kinder and more understanding place.

CHAPTER 14:

Enhancing Emotional Intelligence

Getting better at emotional intelligence is like upgrading your ability to understand and deal with feelings, both yours and others'. Here's a simpler breakdown:

1. Know Your Feelings:

Start by understanding what makes you feel happy, sad, or stressed. Knowing your own emotions is the first step.

2. Handle Stress Well:

Learn ways to deal with stress that work for you – like taking deep breaths, exercising, or taking short breaks. This helps keep your emotions in check.

3. Be Kind and Understanding:

Get better at understanding how others feel. Listen, put yourself in their shoes, and see things from their perspective. It helps you connect better with people.

4. Think Before You Act:

Before doing something or saying something, take a moment to think. Consider how it might affect others. This helps you react in a smarter way.

5. Talk Clearly:

Work on saying what you mean clearly. Good communication is a big part of emotional intelligence. It helps people understand you better.

6. Stay Strong Through Challenges:

Learn to handle tough times without letting them bring you down. Bouncing back after setbacks is a big part of emotional intelligence.

7. Build Good Relationships:

Spend time on relationships that make you feel good. Being a good listener and understanding others helps build strong connections.

8. Learn from Feedback:

Be open to advice. Hearing what others think can help you understand how your actions affect them and how you can improve.

9. Set and Reach Goals:

Set goals that you can actually achieve. Working towards these goals, even small ones, makes you feel good.

10. Stay in the Moment:

Practice staying focused on what's happening now. Things like meditation can help you stay calm and focused.

11. Keep Learning:

Always be curious and keep learning. Understanding emotions and how to handle them is a lifelong journey.

12. Balance Feelings and Thinking:

Find a balance between feelings and logical thinking. Both are important for making good decisions and understanding situations.

13. Stay Positive:

Look at things in a positive way. It doesn't mean ignoring problems but facing them with confidence that you can handle them.

14. Think About Your Actions:

Regularly think about how you act and react. Understanding your own patterns helps you get better at emotional intelligence.

Getting better at emotional intelligence is like a personal journey of growth. It not only makes you feel better but also helps you create positive interactions in your daily life.

PART VIII

Practical Techniques for Investigation

Practical Techniques for Investigation form the backbone of effective inquiry and problem-solving, offering a systematic approach to uncovering information, analyzing data, and reaching informed conclusions. In this exploration, we will delve into a toolkit of practical techniques employed by investigators across various fields, ranging from forensic science to business intelligence. These methods are not just about finding facts but about honing the skills necessary to unravel mysteries, solve puzzles, and make well-informed decisions. Join us on this journey where we unravel the secrets behind the practical techniques that investigators use to navigate the complexities of their investigative pursuits.

Exploring the world of investigation means discovering practical techniques that help uncover secrets and solve puzzles. Whether it's in law, business, or everyday challenges, these techniques are like a toolkit for understanding complicated situations. In our journey, we'll dig into the strategies, tools, and step-by-step processes that investigators use to figure things out. Imagine it as unlocking doors to knowledge and understanding, one method at a time. Come along as we unravel the basics of investigation techniques in a simple and practical way.

CHAPTER 15:

Active Listening

Active listening is like being a listening superhero! It's more than just hearing – it's about really paying attention to what someone is saying. Here's a simpler breakdown:

1. Give Your Full Attention:

   Act like a spotlight on the person talking. Focus on them like they're the main character in a story.

2. Eye Contact:

   Look at them when they talk. It's like saying, "I'm here, and I'm listening."

3. Reflect on What's Said:

   Think about what they said. Respond in a way that shows you understand, like saying, "So, you mean..."

4. Ask Questions:

Be curious! Ask questions to learn more. It's like being a detective gathering clues.

5. Don't Interrupt:

Wait for your turn to talk. Interruptions can be like loud horns in a quiet room. Let them finish first.

6. Use Body Language:

Nod or smile to show you're following along. Your body can speak without words – it's like a silent dance.

7. Feel What They Feel:

Imagine how they're feeling. It's like stepping into their shoes and understanding not just the words but the emotions.

8. Repeat in Your Own Words:

Say it back in your own way. It shows you're not just listening but really getting what they're saying.

9. Stay Focused:

Keep your mind from wandering. Act like you're walking on a tightrope – balancing your focus on the conversation.

10. Suspend Judgment:

Hold off on forming opinions. It's like putting judgment on pause and letting understanding take over.

11. Practice Patience:

Be patient if they need a moment. It's like letting the conversation flow naturally, without rushing.

12. Show You Appreciate:

Say thanks for sharing. Let them know you appreciate them opening up. It's like giving them a little applause.

Active listening is a cool skill that turns regular talks into awesome connections. It's not just about hearing words; it's about understanding, connecting, and making others feel important. So, put on those superhero ears and let the listening adventure begin!

CHAPTER 16:

Questioning Strategies

Questioning strategies are like having different tools for conversations. Let's break it down in simpler terms:

1. Ask Open Questions:

Instead of yes or no questions, ask ones that need more than a short answer. It's like opening a door for more details.

2. Use Probing Questions:

When you want to learn more, use probing questions. They dig deeper, uncovering hidden details, like a conversation detective.

3. Ask Clear Questions:

When things get confusing, ask questions that clear things up. It's like turning on a flashlight in a dark room.

4. Reflect Back:

Repeat what someone said in your own words. It helps them think more about what they're saying.

5. Guide with Leading Questions:

Gently steer the conversation in a certain direction. It's like leaving breadcrumbs for where you want to go.

6. Imagine with Hypothetical Questions:

Ask "what if" questions to explore creative ideas. It's like opening a door to imagination.

7. Narrow Down with Funnel Questions:

Start with a broad question and gradually get more specific. It's like focusing a camera lens.

8. Give Options with Multiple-Choice Questions:

Instead of open-ended questions, offer choices. It helps narrow down possibilities.

9. See Another Side with Reverse Questions:

Flip the question to see things from a different perspective.

10. Use Silence Strategically:

Sometimes, being quiet can encourage others to talk more. It's like giving them space to share.

11. Express Without Words:

Use gestures or pauses to ask questions without speaking. It adds another layer to communication.

12. Summarize at the End:

Wrap up the conversation by summarizing. It ensures everyone understands what was talked about.

These strategies are like tools in a conversation toolbox.

They help you learn more, understand better, and make

talking with others more interesting and meaningful.

CHAPTER 17:

Behavioral Profiling

Behavioral profiling is like figuring out someone's unique way of doing things. It involves looking at the patterns in how people act to understand and predict what they might do. Here's a simpler breakdown:

1. Behavioral Patterns:

Imagine behavior like pieces of a puzzle. Profiling looks at these pieces to see the whole picture of how someone acts in different situations.

2. Establishing Baselines:

Baselines are like starting points. Profiling looks at how someone usually behaves, helping notice when things change.

3. Identifying Triggers:

Triggers are like buttons that influence behavior. Profiling figures out what makes someone act in a certain way, like understanding the reasons behind their actions.

4. Predictive Analysis:

Profiling doesn't just look at the past; it predicts future actions based on what someone has done before.

5. Context Matters:

Behavior happens in certain situations. Profiling considers the environment to understand actions better.

6. Investigative Tool:

In investigations, profiling helps understand why someone did something. It's like a magnifying glass for detectives.

7. Security and Risk Assessment:

Profiling helps assess security risks. In places like airports or online platforms, it helps understand potential threats by looking at behavior.

8. Counter-terrorism and Intelligence:

In stopping terrorism, profiling helps intelligence agencies predict and prevent threats by understanding the behavior of individuals or groups.

9. Psychological Insights:

Profiling gives therapists and psychologists insights into why people do certain things. It's like understanding the reasons behind actions to help people.

10. Ethical Considerations:

Profiling is useful, but it's important to be fair and respect privacy. It's like balancing the benefits of understanding behavior with being respectful.

11. Continuous Evaluation:

Behavior changes over time. Profiling keeps looking at the way people act, updating how we understand them as things change.

12. Decision-Making Support:

In business, profiling helps with decisions. Understanding how employees or customers behave informs strategies to make things work better.

In simple terms, behavioral profiling is like decoding the way people act. It helps us understand patterns, motivations, and even predict what someone might do next. Whether it's in solving crimes, ensuring security, or helping people emotionally, it's a useful tool to understand why people behave the way they do.

PART IX

Ethical Considerations in Understanding Others

Ethical considerations in understanding others form the compass that guides our interactions, ensuring respect, fairness, and responsible engagement. As we embark on the journey of delving into the thoughts, emotions, and behaviors of individuals, it becomes imperative to navigate this exploration with ethical awareness. This introspection not only shapes how we interpret and respond to others but also influences the broader impact of our understanding on relationships, society, and the well-being of individuals. Join us in this exploration of the ethical dimensions that accompany the pursuit of understanding others, recognizing the importance of empathy, respect, and integrity in every step of this enlightening journey.

As we embark on the exploration of understanding others, the significance of ethical considerations becomes increasingly evident. Beyond mere curiosity, this journey involves peering into the intricate fabric of human thoughts, feelings, and actions. Ethical considerations serve as our moral compass, ensuring that this exploration is grounded in principles of respect, fairness, and integrity.

In the pursuit of understanding, we are not just observers but active participants in the lives of others. Every insight gained, every interpretation made, and every interaction forged carries ethical weight. This introspective lens invites us to reflect on the impact of our understanding on individuals, communities, and the broader societal tapestry.

The ethical dimensions of understanding others extend beyond the boundaries of personal relationships into professional realms like psychology, counseling, research, and beyond. It prompts us to consider questions of consent, privacy, and the potential consequences of our insights.

Join us in this exploration as we navigate the intricate terrain of understanding others with ethical sensitivity. Together, let's unravel the threads of empathy, compassion, and responsible engagement, ensuring that our quest for understanding is not only enlightening but also ethically grounded, fostering a culture of respect and dignity.

CHAPTER 18
: **Privacy and Consent**

Respecting people's privacy and getting their permission are like the guardians of good manners when we're trying to understand them. Here's a simpler take:

1. Privacy is Like a Personal Bubble:

Privacy means everyone gets their own space. It's like having a zone where your thoughts and feelings are just yours, and others should respect that.

2. Getting Permission:

Getting permission is like asking if you can join someone's space. It's about making sure they understand and agree before you start exploring their thoughts or feelings.

3. Keeping Secrets Safe:

Keeping secrets is like having a super-secret safe. It means whatever someone shares stays between you and them. This builds trust and makes it okay to talk openly.

4. Balancing Curiosity and Respect:

Learning about others can be like solving a mystery, but it's important to be respectful. Curiosity is good, but it should always respect the limits set by privacy and permission.

5. Different Places, Different Rules:

What's private can change depending on where you are. It's like knowing that what's okay to ask in one place might not be in another. Being aware of these differences is part of being respectful.

6. Taking Care of Some People More:

Some groups, like kids or certain communities, need extra care. It's like being extra cautious and making sure they're comfortable with what you're doing and saying.

7. Locking Up Digital Information:

In the digital world, keeping information safe is like having a strong password. It means making sure that what people share online is protected from others who shouldn't see it.

8. Always Checking In:

Getting permission isn't just a one-time thing; it's ongoing. It's like regularly making sure that everyone is still comfortable and okay with what's happening.

In a nutshell, respecting privacy and asking permission are like the golden rules of understanding others. It's about being polite, making sure everyone feels safe, and creating an environment where people can share without worry.

CHAPTER 19:

Responsible Application of Knowledge

The responsible application of knowledge is like having a powerful tool that comes with a set of guidelines, ensuring that the insights gained and the information gathered are used ethically and for the greater good. Let's delve further into the principles that underpin this responsible application:

1. Ethical Decision-Making:

Responsible application involves considering the ethical implications of using knowledge. It's like having a moral compass that guides decisions, ensuring actions align with principles of fairness, honesty, and integrity.

2. Avoiding Harm:

Imagine knowledge as a double-edged sword. The responsible wielder ensures that the application of knowledge avoids causing harm. It's about being aware of potential negative consequences and taking steps to prevent them.

3. Benefiting Society:

Knowledge becomes a valuable asset when it contributes positively to society. Responsible application seeks to harness knowledge for the greater good, addressing challenges, fostering innovation, and improving overall well-being.

4. Transparency and Accountability:

Responsible use of knowledge involves being transparent about its sources and methods. It's like having an open book – sharing how information was obtained and being accountable for the decisions made based on that knowledge.

5. Contextual Awareness:

Not all knowledge fits every situation. Responsible application involves understanding the context in which knowledge is being applied. It's like recognizing that what works in one scenario may not be suitable in another.

6. Cultural Sensitivity:

Cultural diversity is like a rich tapestry. Responsible application respects and considers different cultural perspectives, ensuring that knowledge is applied in ways that acknowledge and honor diverse beliefs and practices.

7. Continuous Learning:

Knowledge evolves, and responsible application involves a commitment to continuous learning. It's like staying updated on new information, adapting strategies, and ensuring that actions align with the latest insights.

8. Collaboration and Shared Knowledge:

Responsible application encourages collaboration and the sharing of knowledge. It's like recognizing that collective wisdom often leads to better outcomes than individual insights alone.

9. Environmental Stewardship:

The responsible application of knowledge extends to environmental considerations. It's like being a caretaker of the planet, using knowledge to promote sustainability and mitigate negative impacts on the environment.

10. Inclusivity and Accessibility:

Knowledge should be like an open door, accessible to all. Responsible application involves ensuring that knowledge is disseminated inclusively, breaking down barriers and making information available to diverse audiences.

In essence, responsible application is not just about what we know but how we use that knowledge. It's a commitment to ethical conduct, contributing positively to society, and being mindful of the broader impact of our actions. By embracing these principles, we ensure that the power of knowledge is wielded responsibly, fostering a world where insights are a force for good.

PART X

Case Studies

Case studies are like captivating stories that unfold in the real world, offering a detailed exploration of specific situations, challenges, or successes. In this intellectual journey, we immerse ourselves in the complexities of real-life scenarios, dissecting them to understand the nuances, decisions, and outcomes. Case studies serve as invaluable tools across various disciplines, providing a practical lens through which to apply theories, analyze problems, and derive meaningful insights. Join us as we embark on a journey through the realm of case studies, where each story becomes a rich tapestry of lessons, offering a deep dive into the intricacies of practical experiences and their broader implications.

Case studies are like real-life puzzles waiting to be solved. They invite us to dig deep into specific situations, explore the challenges faced, and uncover the strategies that led to success or failure. These studies are not just stories; they are windows into the complexities of the world, offering valuable lessons and insights that go beyond textbook theories.

In the realm of academia, research, and professional analysis, case studies play a pivotal role. They provide a hands-on approach to understanding theories, allowing us to see how they unfold in the messy reality of everyday life. Each case study is a unique narrative, presenting a blend of characters, circumstances, and decisions that contribute to a rich tapestry of knowledge.

Our journey through case studies is an exploration of the practical application of concepts, a journey where theories meet the real world. As we delve into these narratives, we uncover not just what happened but why and how. Join us in this expedition into the heart of case studies, where real stories become invaluable sources of wisdom, guiding us through the twists and turns of genuine experiences.

CHAPTER 20:

Real-world Examples of Investigating Human Psychology

Investigating human psychology through real-world examples is like navigating a fascinating labyrinth of thoughts, emotions, and behaviors. Let's delve deeper into the terrain of understanding human psyche through tangible instances:

1. Therapeutic Case Studies:
   In the realm of therapy, real-world examples provide profound insights into the effectiveness of psychological interventions. Exploring cases where individuals navigate and overcome challenges sheds light on the nuanced processes of healing and personal growth.

2. Criminal Profiling:
   Criminal profiling stands as a real-world application of investigating human psychology. Analyzing criminal cases offers a glimpse into the minds of perpetrators, helping law enforcement understand motivations, patterns, and behavioral characteristics that aid in solving crimes.

3. Marketing and Consumer Behavior:

Investigating consumer behavior in marketing is like decoding the psychology behind purchasing decisions. Real-world examples reveal the impact of advertising, branding, and psychological triggers on consumer choices, shaping the landscape of industries.

4. Workplace Psychology:

Examining workplace dynamics provides practical insights into organizational psychology. Real-world examples showcase the impact of leadership styles, team dynamics, and workplace culture on employee well-being, productivity, and overall success.

5. Educational Psychology:

Real-world examples in educational settings illustrate the application of psychological principles in teaching and learning. Exploring cases of student motivation, cognitive development, and effective teaching strategies contributes to enhancing educational practices.

6. Crisis Intervention:

Investigating human psychology in crisis situations involves real-world scenarios like natural disasters, accidents, or emergencies. Understanding how individuals cope, react, and recover psychologically informs the development of effective crisis intervention strategies.

7. Mental Health Treatment Outcomes:

Real-world examples in mental health settings offer a glimpse into the complexities of treatment outcomes. Examining cases where individuals undergo therapy or psychiatric interventions provides valuable insights into the varied paths of psychological healing.

8. Cross-Cultural Studies:

Investigating human psychology across different cultures unveils the impact of cultural norms and values on psychological processes. Real-world examples showcase how cultural contexts shape beliefs, attitudes, and interpersonal dynamics.

9. Social Media and Online Behavior:

The digital age presents real-world examples of investigating human psychology through online interactions. Studying social media behavior, cyberbullying instances, or the impact of online communities provides insights into the evolving landscape of human connections.

10. Family Dynamics and Counseling:
Real-world examples in family psychology and counseling illuminate the complexities of interpersonal relationships. Exploring cases of familial challenges, dynamics, and interventions offers practical insights into the intricacies of family life.

In essence, investigating human psychology through real-world examples is like having a front-row seat to the intricate dance of the human mind in various contexts. These examples not only enrich our theoretical understanding but also provide a bridge between academic knowledge and the practical intricacies of the human experience.

PART XI

Future Trends in Psycho-social Understanding

The landscape of psycho-social understanding is continually evolving, shaped by emerging trends that cast new light on the intricate interplay between psychological and social factors. In this era of rapid advancements, we stand on the brink of exciting transformations in how we comprehend and address the complexities of human behavior and interaction. Join us on a journey into the future as we explore the promising trends that are poised to redefine psycho-social understanding, unlocking fresh insights into the dynamics of the mind and society. From technological innovations to evolving societal paradigms, these trends hold the potential to revolutionize the way we approach and comprehend the rich tapestry of human experiences.

The horizon of psycho-social understanding is expanding, and the future promises a tapestry woven with innovative threads that will reshape how we perceive and navigate the intricacies of the human mind and social dynamics. As we peer into the future, it becomes evident that transformative trends are poised to usher in a new era of insight and exploration in the realm of psycho-social understanding.

This journey into the future invites us to explore the intersections of psychology and society, guided by the currents of evolving technologies, cultural shifts, and scientific breakthroughs. The landscape is dynamic, with each trend offering a unique vantage point to decode the mysteries of human behavior and relationships.

From the impact of artificial intelligence on mental health interventions to the changing landscapes of social connections in a digitized world, the future trends in psycho-social understanding hold the promise of unveiling novel perspectives and solutions. It is a journey that beckons us to anticipate, adapt, and embrace the unfolding narrative of how we comprehend, support, and enhance the well-being of individuals within the intricate web of societal interactions.

Join us as we embark on an exploration of the future trends that will shape the next chapter in psycho-social understanding, offering a glimpse into a world where knowledge, empathy, and technological advancements converge to illuminate the complex mosaic of the human experience.

CHAPTER 21:

Technological Advances

Imagine technology as a superhero buddy teaming up with psychology to make life cooler. Let's break it down:

1. Chatting with a Therapist Online:

   Now, you can talk to a therapist using your computer or phone. It's like bringing the therapist to your doorstep, even if they're far away.

2. Smart Machines for Mental Health Help:

   Think of smart machines as friendly helpers for your feelings. They can guess how you're doing mentally and offer support to make sure you're okay.

3. Wearable Gadgets Watching Your Feelings:

   There are cool gadgets you can wear like superhero gear. They keep an eye on how you're feeling, checking if you're stressed or need better sleep.

4. Virtual Reality Adventures to Feel Better:

Virtual reality isn't just for games; it's like a magical adventure on a computer to help you feel better, especially when things get tough.

5. Social Media Knowing How Everyone Feels:

Social media isn't just for chatting; it can show how people are feeling. By looking at what people share online, experts can understand trends in how everyone is doing emotionally.

6. Big Data Helping Psychologists Understand Us:

Big data is like a big treasure chest of information. Psychologists use it to study lots of people's behaviors, helping them learn more about why we do the things we do.

7. Making Friends and Getting Support Online:

The internet is not just for fun; it's a place to find friends and support. Online communities let people connect, share experiences, and help each other out. It's like having a big, friendly group online.

8. Apps that Help You Personally:

Some apps are like personal helpers. They understand what you need and give you advice or activities that suit you best. It's like having a little friend in your phone helping you feel good.

9. Watching Your Body and Brain in Action:

Imagine seeing how your body and brain work in real-time. With special gadgets, you can understand and control stress or focus better. It's like having a superpower to make yourself feel calmer or more focused.

10. Being Very Careful with Tech Rules:

While using cool tech, it's super important to follow some important rules. We must make sure everyone's information stays private, ask for permission, and use data in a way that's fair and safe for everyone.

So, technology is like a buddy that makes life more fun and easier. But, just like superheroes, we need to use it in a way that keeps everyone safe and happy.

CHAPTER 22:

Interdisciplinary Approaches

Interdisciplinary approaches are like forming a superhero squad of experts from different fields. They join forces to tackle big problems and understand tricky things. Here's a simpler breakdown:

1. Building a Dream Team:

Imagine putting together a team with experts from different areas, like puzzle masters, problem solvers, and tech whizzes.

2. Solving Real Problems:

Instead of just talking about problems, this team works on real-world issues. It's like having a toolbox with lots of different tools, and each expert brings their special tool to fix things properly.

3. Seeing the Full Picture: Instead of looking at problems bit by bit, the team checks from different angles. It's like using

different colored glasses to see the whole picture, understanding how different things fit together.

4. Sharing Knowledge:

Everyone in the team learns from each other. It's like a big knowledge swap – the brainiacs share what they know about people, tech, and society.

5. Understanding Everything:

Instead of only looking at a piece, the team wants to know everything about a problem. It's like seeing a big painting with lots of details, getting the full story.

6. Connecting Different Subjects:

The team connects different areas that might not seem related. It's like linking up the dots between studying people's minds, using tech, or understanding how societies work.

7. Thinking Up New Stuff:

   The team doesn't just talk; they come up with new ideas.

It's like mixing up ingredients to create something special,

making things better and cooler.

8. Using Ideas in Real Life:

   What the team thinks up isn't just for talking – they use it in

the real world. It's like taking cool ideas from studying people,

adding tech, and making things like apps to help everyone.

9. Breaking Down School Subjects:

   Instead of keeping ideas in separate areas, the team

mixes them up. It's like getting rid of imaginary walls

between subjects in school, letting everything flow together.

10. Fixing Big World Problems:

   The team isn't just solving small problems; they're tackling

huge ones. It's like a superhero group taking on big

challenges like fixing the Earth, making everyone healthy, or making the world fair for everyone.

In simple terms, interdisciplinary approaches are like a cool team-up where experts from different areas work together to figure out tough problems and make the world a better place. They bring their own special skills to the table, like superheroes with unique powers, and together, they create solutions for big challenges.

PART XII

Conclusion

In the captivating journey of how to understand the human psychology, we've explored the intricate realms of cognition, behavior, and emotions. From the exploration of cognitive processes to the application of technological advances, our pursuit has been akin to unraveling the mysteries of a complex tapestry. Interdisciplinary approaches have illuminated the path, showing that collaboration among diverse fields enhances our grasp of human experiences.

As we navigate through real-world examples and anticipate future trends, the essence remains clear – the study of human psychology is dynamic, evolving, and profoundly impactful. It extends beyond textbooks and reaches into the core of our interactions, guiding us to comprehend, connect, and support one another. In this ongoing expedition, the fusion of knowledge, empathy, and innovative approaches propels us toward a deeper understanding of ourselves and the intricate fabric of human existence.

CHAPTER 23:

Summarizing Key Takeaways

Let's sum up what we've learned about understanding people's minds in a simpler way:

1. Thinking and Patterns:

We explored how our minds work, looking at how we think and the ways we solve problems.

2. Spotting Tricky Thoughts:

We learned about tricky ways our minds can fool us, emphasizing the need to think carefully and know ourselves better.

3. Cool Tech Helping Minds:

We saw how awesome technology, like talking to therapists online and using smart gadgets, can make our minds feel better.

4. Teamwork of Experts:

Teaming up experts from different areas helps solve real problems, showing that working together brings a better understanding of how people behave.

5. Real-life Stories:

Stories from real life, like solving crimes or studying how people feel, showed how psychology is everywhere, affecting different parts of our lives.

6. Looking Ahead:

We peeked into the future, imagining exciting changes like using more technology, learning from new trends, and keeping in mind important rules about using information responsibly.

7. Being Fair and Responsible:

We always remembered to be fair and careful, especially when using technology, respecting people's privacy, and making sure everyone is okay.

So, the big picture is about understanding people better, using technology wisely, and working together to solve real problems – a journey that never stops, full of discoveries and ways to make our lives and the world a bit better.

CHAPTER 24:
Encouraging Continuous Learning in Human Psychology

Encouraging continuous learning in human psychology is like opening a door to endless exploration and understanding. Let's delve deeper into why embracing a mindset of ongoing discovery is crucial in this dynamic field:

1. Ever-Changing Landscape:

Human psychology is not static; it evolves with society, technology, and cultural shifts. Continuous learning ensures staying abreast of the latest developments, trends, and insights that shape our understanding of the human mind.

2. Adapting to New Research:

New studies and research findings constantly emerge, offering fresh perspectives on human behavior. Embracing continuous learning allows professionals and enthusiasts to adapt their knowledge base to incorporate these cutting-edge insights.

3. Technological Advancements:

The integration of technology with psychology is a rapidly evolving frontier. Continuous learning is essential to harness the potential of new tools, from virtual therapies to AI applications, and to understand their impact on psychological understanding.

4. Interdisciplinary Insights:

Interdisciplinary collaboration introduces new ways of thinking and problem-solving. Embracing continuous learning fosters an openness to interdisciplinary approaches, enriching one's understanding by incorporating diverse perspectives from various fields.

5. Enhancing Therapeutic Practices:

For mental health professionals, ongoing learning ensures the incorporation of the latest therapeutic approaches and interventions. This continuous improvement is vital for providing effective and up-to-date support to individuals seeking psychological help.

6. Cultural Sensitivity:

Human psychology is deeply influenced by cultural nuances. Continuous learning allows practitioners to stay culturally sensitive, understanding the diverse factors that shape behavior and ensuring that psychological interventions are tailored to different cultural contexts.

7. Navigating Ethical Challenges:

The field of psychology often grapples with ethical considerations. Staying informed through continuous learning equips professionals with the knowledge to navigate ethical challenges responsibly, maintaining the highest standards of practice.

8. Teaching and Mentoring:

Those involved in teaching or mentoring others in psychology benefit immensely from continuous learning. It allows educators to transmit the most current and relevant knowledge to the next generation of psychologists, fostering a culture of intellectual growth.

9. Personal and Professional Growth:

Continuous learning is a pathway to personal and professional growth. Whether through workshops, conferences, or staying updated with literature, the pursuit of knowledge in psychology enhances one's skills, expertise, and overall effectiveness.

10. Fostering Curiosity and Innovation:

A mindset of continuous learning nurtures curiosity and innovation. It encourages asking new questions, exploring novel methodologies, and pushing the boundaries of conventional thinking within the field of psychology.

In essence, encouraging continuous learning in human psychology is not just about staying informed; it's about fostering a mindset of curiosity, adaptability, and a genuine passion for unraveling the complexities of the human mind. It transforms the journey of understanding psychology into a dynamic and ever-enriching exploration.

www.ingramcontent.com/pod-product-compliance
Lightning Source LLC
Chambersburg PA
CBHW070805260726
48660CB00005B/1711